How to Be a Great Boss

Also by Mack Munro

How to Win at Performance Management

BossTalk: What Every Boss Needs to Know to About Giving Great Presentations

How to Build Better Bosses

How to Build an Engaged Workforce

How to Be a Great Boss

By
Mack Munro

KDP . Vanleer, TN

© 2019 by Mack Munro. All rights reserved (3/2019)

How to Be a Great Boss

Published by KDP

No part of this publication may be reproduced, stored in a retrieval system or transmitted in any form or by any means, electronic, mechanical, photocopying, recording, scanning or otherwise, except as permitted under code 107 or 108 of the 1976 United States Copyright Act, without the prior written permission of the Author. Requests to the Author for permission should be addressed to Main Line Press, P.O. Box 75, Vanleer, TN 37181.

Printed in the United States of America

ISBN: 9781090333230

Quantity discounts are available on bulk purchases of this book for educational training purposes, fund-raising, or gift giving. For more information, contact us at the address below. Special books, booklets, or book excerpts can also be created to fit your specific needs. For more information, contact Marketing Department
P.O. Box 75, Vanleer, TN 37181.

Table of Contents

Prologue	7
Chapter 1: The Problem Unveiled	13
Chapter 2: Inside, Not Outside	25
Chapter 3: Listen Up!	29
Chapter 4: Are Those My Shoes?	33
Chapter 5: Get Real!	37
Chapter 6: Get Off My Back!	41
Chapter 7: Show Me the Money?	43
Chapter 8: Get a Grip	47
Chapter 9: Do You Have a Life?	51
Chapter 10: Are You Emotional?	55
Chapter 11: Are You a Know-it-All?	59
Chapter 12: I'm Not You	63
Chapter 13: Throw in the Towel!	67
About the Author	71
About Boss Builder Academy	73

Prologue

"If we are asked to describe what a good manager is, everybody seems to be able to come up with an answer. We read about what skills make good managers and drive our conclusions about what managers should not be doing. But are we really able to respond to this question until we experience the reality? The relationship with our manager or supervisor has a much bigger impact on our emotional and physical health than any other relationships at work. Personally, I did not fully understand this until I ended up with one of the 'bad' managers myself. It took two years to lose most of my self-confidence, my motivation, and achievement drive.

I ended up at the doctor's office suffering from insomnia and anxiety - conditions that are common in the workplace today. It was no comfort to find out that two of my colleagues, reporting to the same manager, suffered from the same conditions. It is even harder to believe that this manager was the person in charge of management development initiatives at the company. What did I learn from this experience? It is one thing to read about what makes successful managers. The real challenge though is to apply what you read in everyday life. To be a successful manager it is essential to learn to manage yourself, your own emotions, your strengths and weaknesses and to be able to *listen to others and be aware of their feelings, needs and concerns."*

Kind of a depressing start for a book isn't it?

This story, told several years ago by a good friend and colleague is the main reason I focus my work on creating good bosses. Years of both working for, and observing bad bosses myself pushed me to focus on organizational and management development as a career. One aspect particularly intrigues me: the development of new or aspiring managers. You know them as The Boss.

It's important to figure out just what we're supposed to do as The Boss. In my experience, most new bosses are hired from the ranks of technical experts. I guess the rationale is that if they are great technicians, they'll also be great bosses. Unfortunately, without some sort of clarification and development, that won't happen. I'd like to suggest three key areas a manager must master to be a great boss.

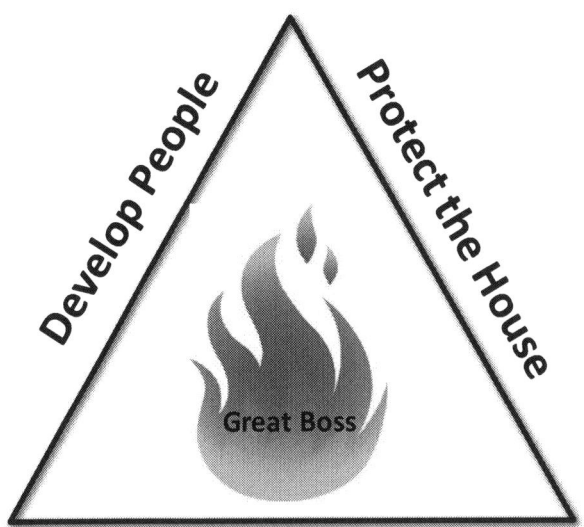

Fix Systems/Processes

Area #1: Fixing Systems and Processes

This is a no-brainer. We create new bosses from the ranks of those who are expert problem-solvers and process-fixers. It's a good thing too since these folks will be staffing the department and be there to impart their wisdom. Plus, people tend to respect a boss who at least knows a little bit more than they do.

Area #2: Protecting the House

The Boss also needs to be on the lookout for any potential danger either from an OSHA standpoint or an HR standpoint. This means every decision The Boss makes must consider liabilities because The Boss eventually owns it. This is why it's important to pay attention to all that boring HR compliance training.

Area #3: Developing People

This is the part that scares most new managers. Developing people means monitoring their performance and providing coaching and feedback. It's also the area where managers make the biggest excuses.

"I don't have time to coach my employees. I'm always putting out fires."

It's counter-intuitive. If you spent the time to develop, there would be fewer fires to put out!

If you're a new manager, it's important to set up a development plan to grow in all three of those crucial areas. You'll naturally get better fixing systems and processes as that's something you do each day. Becoming a student in the HR areas is a great way to protect the house. Partnering with HR and taking time on your own to read up on current trends and even going to monthly HR meetings is a good place to start. For developing others, formal training (like our Boss Builder Academy) is absolutely necessary. Finding a good mentor and doing your own reading, podcast-listening, and blog reading. Go to ***www.BossBuilderBlog.com*** for good articles will benefit you. Our podcast, The Boss Builder Podcast (available on *iTunes, Google Play, Spotify,* and *Stitcher* and at **www.BossBuilderPodcast.com**) is a great source of information too.

For all the complexity in organizations today, it's very easy to nail down the management issue – it's a lack of people skills. While it's easy to give solutions, results take work (lots of personal and professional development.) This kind of development won't come automatically. It takes lots of work and a commitment to do it right. The principles in this book aren't a panacea, but they sure give you a place to start.

Remember, having this three-phased foundation is just the start. There is much to learn and this book will give you 12 strategies and a 10 item Daily Checklist that can build on your foundation. Take some time to read and reflect and you'll be well on your way to being a Great Boss!

ps. The last few pages has a nine week reflection. Be sure to list the things you will either START, STOP, CONTINUE, or CHANGE as you grow!

Difference Between

 Boss   &   Leader

Boss	Leader
Gets things done	...Thinks about getting things done
Doesn't tolerate poor performers	...Wastes time trying to rehab poor performers
Focuses on the bottom line	...Reflects on everything BUT the bottom line
Has a profit-based mindset	...Wonders why the business isn't growing
Does the right things right	...Reads books about the right things to do
Commands	...Asks
Takes the credit AND the blame	...Agonizes over who would be most appropriate to get the credit

While the leaders are trying to figure out how to be more popular and visionary, the boss is growing the business.
Be the boss. That takes work. Anyone can be a leader.

What do you think?

Chapter 1 – The Problem Unveiled

The Boss holds a significant role in the climate of the workplace. As Americans, we average about 47 hours per week at work, so the time managers spend as an influence in our lives is really second only to that of a typical parent-child relationship.

Each of us probably remembers bosses we really enjoyed working for. Of course, there were also some bosses we remember for other, more negative reasons. Perhaps we saw them as incompetent. Maybe they treated us with contempt. In some cases, we adapted to the bad bosses, but going to work was most likely an event we dreaded. In other cases, we probably made the decision to leave as soon as possible. This choice is not unique. Most employee surveys say the **NUMBER ONE** reason employees gave for leaving the organization was "dissatisfaction with their supervisors". That's huge!

Certainly the fault doesn't lie entirely with The Boss. For the most part, they are overworked, underpaid, and deal with a mountain of tasks and stress that only seems to increase. What exactly are managers supposed to do? I've asked this question many times, both in my college courses and when facilitating workshops in different organizations. *Figure 1* shows some of a manager's tasks, roles, and responsibilities. The list is daunting (and this is only a fraction of what I gathered!):

What Managers Do

• Hire Staff	• Work With People
• Lead and Manage	• Communicate
• Budget	• Teach
• Motivate (Provide Incentives)	• Empower
• Human Resource Management (Relationship)	• Reach Goals & Objectives
	• Problem Solve
• Cohesion	• Conflict Resolution
• Communicate	• Decision-Making
• Organize	• Planning & Training
• Troubleshoot	• Obtaining Resources
• Mentor	• Listen to Whining
• Evaluate	• Go To Meetings
• Make It Better	• Share Information
• Delegate	• Teambuilding
• Prioritize	• Group Identification
• Watch	• Group Participation
• Train	• Observe And Give Feedback
• Work	• Be Visible
• Reports/Paperwork	• Ensure Workflow Is Carried Out To Get Things Accomplished
• Educate	
• Facilitate Change	
• Support The Mission	• Staff Training
• Prioritize Department Goals	• Set The Vision
• Discipline	• Communicate Up And Down
• Coordinate	
• Safe Environment	• Plan For The Future
• Plan	• Fiscal And Materials Management
• Role Model	
• Leadership	• Evaluate
• Rock Moving	• Talk On The Phone
• Cheerleading	• Meetings
	• Read E-Mail
	• Fill in for staff

Figure 1

That's quite a list, and most of it takes place before lunch! As The Boss, we work as hard as we can to please OUR boss, employees, customers, and co-workers only to find out that NOBODY is happy with us! The extra pay just doesn't go far enough. In spite of all the material written about management, and the wide range of training programs available, the problem continues.

I don't believe management is the root cause of people problems, but in many ways it has become a chronic contributor. Why? I have two theories:

No Formal Development Process

We have detailed manuals on programming and maintaining computers. Employees are put through rigorous training programs to learn the latest accounting and management software. We spend thousands of dollars gaining certifications in various technical fields. But ironically, in order to manage the most intricate, sensitive, difficult, yet productive, invaluable, and hard to find part of our organization – PEOPLE, we simply promote the most qualified technical person and let them figure it out on their own!

Think about it! Would you ever let a novice computer technician take down and re-configure your server without so much as a *Book for Dummies*? Would you allow rookie warehouse workers to operate a forklift without at least giving them some basic safety instructions? *Then why in the world are managers allowed to plan, organize, direct, and control PEOPLE without so much as an introductory class in human behavior?*

More Value Placed on Productivity and Position than People

Managers are traditionally recognized and rewarded for maximizing production, turning out numbers, and "getting the job done." The "soft skills" such as staff development, performance management (to some extent) and other "people issues" are either downplayed or relegated to random times when managers can actually devote some effort toward them. Additionally, managers also must involve themselves in the politics of an organization in order to effectively allocate resources, or to ensure the top brass notices their division. Most of what is seen as managerial *success* may not equate to what is deemed managerial *effectiveness*.

In 1988, a researcher named Fred Luthans and some of his associates began examining the role of management from a non-traditional perspective. They made an overall distinction between managers who were seen as *effective*, and those who were seen as *successful*. *Success* was defined as moving up the corporate ladder quickly and *effectiveness* was described as doing a good job, as well as having the satisfaction and commitment of their employees. Luthans surveyed more than 450 managers and found that generally, managers all work in and out of four main activities:

Traditional Management	Decision-making, planning, controlling
Communication	Exchanging routine information and processing paperwork
Human Resource Management	Motivating, disciplining, managing conflict, staffing, training
Networking	Socializing, politics, interacting with outsiders

Luthans categorized managers three ways: **Average**, **Successful**, and **Effective**. He then detailed what percent of time each manager spent in the four managerial activities. His study concluded the following:

Manager	Traditional	Communication	HRM	Networking
Average	32%	29%	20%	19%
Successful	13%	28%	11%	48%
Effective	19%	44%	26%	11%

The study showed what many people seem to understand: It's not always **WHAT** you know, it's **WHO** you know. Actually that's a bit simplistic and doesn't accurately describe the findings. But the study revealed that those managers who spent a significant amount of time networking managed to attain a level of success much quicker than those who spent the majority of their time doing traditional management activities and communicating with their employees. I'm sure we all remember certain managers who we really liked and respected but somehow never seemed to be promoted to where **we** thought they should be. Conversely, we probably also know some managers, who, in our minds, have no business being at the level they are. The reward systems simply don't value the human element nearly enough at the managerial level.

Where Did We Go Wrong?

To answer this question, you must take a look at the management development trends of the past 100 years. One major reason we have the people issues at work today, is we're attempting to manage people as if we were maintaining machinery, and this is in spite of the fact that studies done in the last 50 years alone prove that people are a lot more intricate and sensitive than machines!

So What?

By looking at the last 100 years, we see that our attempts to depersonalize and dehumanize the work environment have led to failure. With the Baby Boomers ready to leave the work environment, and younger generations now dominating, a new emphasis must be made on using better people skills.

Managers need to develop their interpersonal skills if they're going to be effective in their jobs. Companies with reputations as good places to work get them in a large part by having managers who take good care of their people.

This gives them a decided advantage when trying to attract and retain good employees.

Frequent studies of the U.S. workforce find that:

- Wages and fringe benefits are not the reason people like their jobs or stay with an employer

- Job quality and the supportiveness of the work environment are most important to workers.

If managers have good interpersonal skills, the work environment should feel more supportive and pleasant, which in turn makes it easier to hire and retain high performing employees.

Managers are also faced with several challenges as we move at lightning speed through the 21st century. **Figure 3** shows just a few examples of the complexity managers face today:

Figure 3

Responding to Globalization

With more and more companies being purchased by foreign companies, and with the trend toward global trade growing, managers will be faced with new challenges in dealing with different people from different cultures.

Workforce Diversity

The make-up of today's workforce is more diverse than ever. Older workers are staying longer, immigrants are increasing in greater numbers, and the balance of women in the workplace is increasing.

Work/Life Balance Conflicts

Americans work an average of 47 hours per week. This increase puts a strain on the lives of both employee and manager.

Customer Service and People Skills

Currently, the majority of U.S. workers are employed in service jobs. With our society increasing the number of service jobs, having better customer service and people skills may be what keeps your organization viable over the next few years.

Responding to Labor Shortages

If current trends continue, the United States will have a labor shortage for the next 10-15 years (particularly in skilled positions). Attracting and keeping good employees will be one of management's greatest challenges.

Empowering People

Current trends in management blur the lines between management and employees. Teams and groups are becoming more popular and are changing the role of manager from "boss" to "facilitator".

Stimulating Change and Innovation

Companies that maintain flexibility, continually improve quality, and beat their competition to the marketplace with innovative products and services, will be tomorrow's winners.

Improving Quality and Productivity

A new emphasis on quality requires buy-in and cooperation from employees. Managers are facing a significant challenge here, as they must realize a new role: that of *Salesperson and Cheerleader!*

Temporariness

Both individuals and organizations are faced with changing trends, which require rapid upsizing and downsizing. Lifelong employment with one company rarely exists anymore.

And Your Point is?

I see the next few years as an opportunity for great bosses to emerge! There is a new generation entering the workforce that in many ways possesses the knowledge, skills, and attitudes to make both YOU as The Boss, and your organization succeed. **The key is to get to understand them, learn how to motivate them, and then take up the challenge of leading them to a brighter future.** While this book is a roadmap to getting there, it takes a commitment from YOU to make it happen.

Please take the time to both read and embrace the principles in this book. They're all very simple, but that doesn't mean they're easy. Each one will take an action plan, patience, and lots of work, but I promise you'll reap the benefits a hundred times over. Your staff will see you in a new light. Their performance will improve. You'll have more time for performance management and employee development. Since they're now working harder and smarter, you'll have more down time to refresh your mind.

There's plenty of benefit here for you. Take the principles to heart and your performance as The Boss will blossom!

"The worst manager I had was one that cursed and acted like a child when they were unable to have their way. This manager was famous for changing your name, if they could not pronounce it and expected you to answer and if you didn't answer, this manager would go off into a whole new world--negative world. This manager wanted everything right then and there, even if the request was out-of-reach, that didn't matter. This manager felt everyone should bow down each and every time they entered the room. This manager had no clue as to how the office was being ran nor the roles of the associates. This job was given to this manager because of who they knew, not because of what they knew--bad management."

D. E.

Chapter 2 – Inside, not Outside

One of my all-time favorite TV shows was *Fear Factor*. If you're not familiar with this program, contestants competed in a series of stunts designed to play off their greatest fears. There's usually a "height" stunt, a "water" stunt, and then of course the "eating" stunt – which is my personal favorite. Contestants are shown an apparently harmless, tasty-looking treat only to be informed that it's crawling with roaches or worms or something equally disgusting on the inside, and of course they have to eat it. If you watched *Fear Factor* enough, you knew not to judge the stunt on the outward appearance.

So why do we do that on a regular basis with people in our lives? Our tendency is to operate on the surface level with others, making judgments on what we see rather than who they are. We look at someone's background, education level, experiences, and body language and make a conscious choice with that data to treat them one way or another. It's a fancy statement for stereotyping isn't it? Even the more savvy of us try to group individuals together with personality assessments and indicators hoping to better understand others, but simply do the same thing.

So what's the answer?

Get to know individuals individually. There are no two human beings that are totally identical. Geneticists say that the probability of finding your EXACT double is 2×10^{32}. In other words, you'll never find it. Each individual has unique needs, wants, motivations, personalities, values, experiences, and gifts. We can't discern those from the outward appearance any more than we can figure out what disgusting creatures are squirming inside of the food on *Fear Factor*.

Take the time to talk to your people. Allow them to tell their story. Learn to appreciate their unique gifts. Find out what motivates them both extrinsically and intrinsically. You might be surprised at what wonderful, talented people you have working for you.

Anyone can judge on the outward appearance. Differentiate yourself here and you'll be well on your way to becoming a great manager and leader.

Points to Ponder

1. Take a look inside yourself – who are you?

2. Think of three people you know well. Identify characteristics you know but others would never based on their outward appearance.

3. Make it a point to meet 3 new strangers a day. Get to know them at a deeper level.

4. Think about why you make a judgment based on outward appearance – where did that come from? Can you change it?

5. Think about three figures from history – could people have made incorrect assumptions based on how they appeared on the outside?

6. What are three strategies you can employee today to help you focus on the inward rather than the outward appearance? Where can you apply them?

> "I was in management for a worldwide telemarketing company. The call center director and I did not see eye to eye on everything. I however did my job and did it well and with professionalism. My husband was having a major operation. I had time off and had saved it for this upcoming operation. She denied me the time off. She was missing a heart. Perhaps she had it removed. LOL."
>
> C. B.

Chapter 3 – Listen Up!

We just learned the value of looking on the inside with Principle #1. Principle #2 gives you some insight on how to do that.

Be a good listener.

Ok, we've all heard that one before. "God gave you two ears and only one mouth so use them in that priority." But how can we really take steps to be good listeners?

In order to be a better communicator and to have those around us feel totally heard and understood, we have to practicing active listening. Active listening is more than hearing what people say and goes beyond just looking them in the eyes (although both practices are important). Active listening means practicing a deep level of discernment. It involves listening for subtleties below the surface; subtleties like needs and emotions.

Why are needs and emotions so important to listen for?

While some people seem to talk just to hear the sound of their own voice, most people communicate in order to get something. Needs and emotions are usually good indicators of what people want. Needs are the substances that fill voids. It could be a physical need such as food or water. It might be an emotional need such as an opportunity to vent or receive empathy. It can even be a spiritual need such as a yearning to connect to a higher power. Needs are different that wants ("I want a new Mercedes") in that they indicate something deeper (i.e. "I want the Mercedes to give me a feeling of reward for all the hard work I did in building my career"). If we listen for, and identify needs, we can then offer suggestions, advice, or even give tangibles that really help the listener get satisfaction.

Listening for emotions first involves identifying emotions. Emotions are more than sadness and the tugging of your heart when viewing the ending of *Old Yeller*. Emotions can also include anger, rage, elation, and a whole range of other feelings. Sometimes we have to sort through emotions to hear the real message. Other times we might just hear what we need from the emotions themselves.

By practicing the skills of active listening, you'll find people become drawn to you and begin asking for your opinions and advice. By being a good listener, you'll even encourage your employees to find solutions to their own dilemmas because the answer might become apparent to them when they speak with you without interruption. It's a key people skill and one that will benefit you both at work and in your personal relationships. It won't be easy – plan on spending many hours practicing, but the results are well worth the effort.

Points to Ponder

1. How good are you at listening for needs? What can you do right now to improve that ability?

2. How good are you at listening for emotions? What can you do right now to improve that ability?

3. Think about a time you felt listened to. What helped you feel listened to?

4. Identify someone who you think is a good listener. What are three things they do to make you feel listened to?

5. Identify three things you do that may tell your staff you're not fully tuned it when they talk. What can you do to change that behavior?

> "I had a manager who qualified as the worst manager ever. Among other things he had a habit of taking credit for my work. He did it constantly to make himself look good to the director. Eventually a new director took over and removed him from the position. Yes, I got the position and never saw that manager again."
>
> C. T.

Chapter 4 – Are Those My Shoes?

Principle #3 is one of the most basic acts we can do but leads to incredible success: putting ourselves in our employees' shoes.

Stephen Covey referred to this as one of his *7 Habits* in the principle "Seek first to understand, then be understood." He's absolutely right. Did you know that each of your employees are completely different? They all have different experiences, values, attitudes, wants, needs, desires, and goals. Each day these influence their work life and they can't help but be affected by them. As a manager, you have absolutely no control on how these folks feel on the inside. Your only hope is to reverse roles with them and see things from their perspective and current state of mind.

Think about how you feel when someone invalidates your opinion, experience, or feelings. You probably get a sense of hurt followed by apathy or anger. If you continually manage without ever taking time to see a different perspective, this probably explains why your employees withdraw from you or at the very least don't trust you.

This is a learned skill that takes a great amount of practice. It involves active listening and careful reflective communication. You might be tempted when developing this skill to say something like this to a distraught employee:

I know how you feel.

Resist this. Do you really know how they feel? Why not try this instead:

That's a real difficult situation you're in. It sounds as though you're very frustrated (or angry, sad, scared etc). *Is that correct?*

Allow them to respond and listen carefully to their response. They'll either validate it or deny it. Continue to probe using your active listening skills. Let them tell you when you've got it right. Then you can move on and continue the conversation from a perspective they'll be comfortable with. By developing this skill, you'll open up the door to better communication with your employees and go a long way to improving your relationships with others.

It's going to take work. You'll have to resist the temptation to rush to judgment. You'll need to be patient with both yourself and your employees, but it's worth the effort. Just another tool in your toolbox, but it's an important one! Take some time to put it into practice.

Points to Ponder

1. How good are you at listening for needs and emotions? What can you do right now to improve that ability?

2. Do you rush to judgment when listening to an employee share their problems with you? If so, why?

3. Think about a time you felt listened to when you had a major crisis in your life. What helped you feel listened to?

4. Has anyone ever shot down a good idea you had? How did that make you feel? Do you find yourself doing the same thing to your employees?

5. Identify someone who you think is a good listener. What are three things they do to make you feel listened to?

"I had this manager that I really could not deal with. This person was very negative, didn't have people skills and could not relate to any of their co-workers. One day this person would be happy and laughing with one day and the next day that person would have a attitude the next morning. I came to realize that this person was having alot of personal problems at home, and could not separate their personal when they come to work the next day. I feel that this is one big problem with managers they can not separate their personal problems and not take it out on their co-workers..."

K. H.

Chapter 5 – Get Real!

If you've managed to remember and learn the first three principles, take a moment and think before you brag about it – Principle #4 could be written for you:

Be humble – nobody is good enough to be arrogant!

When a wide receiver makes a spectacular catch and taunts the defensive back in the end zone does that tick you off? Do you cringe when you watch old footage of Muhammad Ali proclaiming, "I'm the greatest?"

Although both athletes truly are remarkable, it's their arrogance that most people think of when reflecting back on their careers. Of course arrogance isn't isolated to just athletics. I've worked with and around plenty of folks throughout my career that displayed similar characteristics.

But shouldn't we be confident? After all nobody wants to hang around people with low self-esteem.

Of course we should be confident! But there's a big difference between confidence and arrogance. Confidence comes from within. You feel it, and others can sense it. Arrogance starts from within, but others are forced into experiencing it. Let me give you an example.

One of my former co-workers was surprised one day when an NFL legend from the 1960s visited our office for a meeting with the Executive Director. On his way out, he stopped by the front desk and asked her if she wanted his autographed photo before he left! Now I always thought it was the fan who asked for the autograph, but I guess it's not always the case.

When a friend of mine wrote his first book, he asked me what he should do when people asked him to sign it. He is a very humble guy – very experienced and has lots of knowledge, but he'll never brag about it. He said he felt kind of funny autographing books, but I told him that if he was asked, then he should do it, but never offer to sign – it could come off as a little arrogant.

Arrogance really harms a workplace. If you think back on the worse boss you ever had, I'm sure there was just a hint of arrogance somewhere driving the bad behavior you remembered. As a manager, don't fall into the arrogance trap. You're never too good to clean up after yourself, make your own coffee (and some for your staff as well), or admit you're wrong. We're paid to work for you, not worship you.

So the question is, who really can afford to be arrogant? After all, we all have flaws. I for one have failed at many things. Personally, I'm a lot more comfortable being around people who admit mistakes, flaws, failures, and disappointments because I then look at their success and appreciate it more. They seem more real and personable to me. They get my respect not because of what they do, but who they are. They don't ask for respect, but I really want to give it to them.

Strive for excellence. Be the very best at what you do. Achieve your goals and help others do the same. But do this with confidence, not arrogance. Let others raise you up, don't do it yourself. Keep your ego in check and watch how the world promotes you. It's much better than having to do it yourself!

Points to Ponder

1. Has anyone ever told you that you were arrogant? What might have given them that perception?

2. Think of someone whose accomplishments you admire. Are they arrogant? If so, does that change your opinion about them?

3. What are some of the greatest accomplishments in your life? Can you identify people that helped you achieve them? Have you thanked them lately?

The worst manager takes credit for my thoughts and ideas.

I was working at a radio station and they had just moved into the local market here. As they were getting the market setup and hiring sales people and other managers, I would see areas that could use improvement. Such as creating the sales order form online so we would not have so much paper. When I presented the idea to the district manager, he totally shot me down, and you know I was cool with it. Then two weeks later his boss is down visiting to see how we were doing and I over here the district manager saying that he thought we should put the sales order online to save paper! I was in shock. I immediately began looking for a new job.

V. T.

Chapter 6 – Get Off My Back!

Each term when I began the *Intro to Management* course I taught at a local university, I asked my students to share stories about the worst manager they ever worked for. It never ceased to amaze me what kinds of behaviors they describe. The call-out boxes at the end of each chapter in this book tells some of their stories. I do however see one specific behavior that pops up in every discussion: micromanagement.

I'm not even sure if this term is a real word or not but it might as well be. It's a noun, a verb, and in some ways perhaps an expletive. I guess it means a manager who needs to double and triple check their subordinate's process each step of the way. In other words, they can't fully trust them to complete a task without having their stamp of approval at regular intervals.

Now before we beat these folks up, I guess we should attempt to discover why this happens. It could be they were burned in the past – after all, you can delegate authority, but never responsibility. It could be a part of their personality. Maybe they were mentored by a micromanager. But at some point, I think we need to examine the reason and break the cycle.

Did you know most employees are good workers who would probably forego a pay raise for just a little autonomy? All of us need to feel some sense of control. We're all born with some natural skills and abilities and if we're given a chance to use them to the best of OUR abilities, we'll probably be able to grow. I'm convinced that there is really no such thing as a bad employee. If someone is not measuring up performance-wise, it might just be a bad fit with their skills. The answer is to MOVE THEM! Allow them to work within their skills sets (if possible) and then take your hands off and see how they perform. The best employees will only get better if you take this approach.

So this week, think about what you can do to unleash the skills of your employees. Keep an eye on them of course, but give them a chance and you might be surprised how well they'll do.

Points to Ponder

1. Are you a micromanager? Have you been called a micromanager before?

2. Do you delegate tasks frequently? Are they significant or menial? Do you follow up frequently on the progress?

3. What scares you about delegation? How can you conquer that fear?

Chapter 7 – Show Me The Money?

One of the most common complaints I hear from managers is that they need some way to motivate their employees, but the budget doesn't allow for raises. Without the ability to give a bonus or a raise, they feel powerless.

I have news for them (and you): **It's Not Always About the Money!**

What people don't realize is that in many cases, what troubles people about a job and leads to a lack of motivation isn't the pay or benefits necessarily, but maybe the job itself. Think back on the worst job you ever had. Chances are that it wasn't the pay that annoyed you, it was most likely the boss you had (see Points #4 and #5) or the job itself. Maybe it wasn't challenging. Perhaps you felt a lack of recognition or growth. If that was the case, you had no job satisfaction.

This isn't a new discovery. Back in the 1950s, a researcher named Frederick Herzberg did some studies that proved an interesting point: there is a difference between having job satisfaction and having job dissatisfaction. Job satisfaction centered around a challenging job, upward mobility, and the intrinsic rewards of the job itself. Job dissatisfaction came from poor pay and benefits and perhaps an unsafe environment. These are mutually exclusive.

You can't solve a job satisfaction problem with a job dissatisfaction solution.

What does this mean?

If you hate your job right now because the pay is low, then getting more responsibility or some recognition won't help you. Conversely, if you find the pay satisfactory but you feel like you're in a dead end job, a pay raise or bonus will only provide a temporary burst of motivation. If this is the case for you, then imagine what your employees are going through. Can you tell the difference in them?

So here's your challenge this week. Take a look at the people who work for you. See if you can identify those who love their job, those who are dissatisfied with their job, and those who have no job satisfaction. Now that you know the difference between the last two, you can take steps to meet their needs. If you don't have money to pay them more, take a hard look at the reason they're unhappy. Is it a satisfaction problem? Ask them what would make the job more attractive. Find their "sweet spot" – the button you can push to positively motivate them. See if you can put them on a track for promotion. Allow them to take on a new challenge in an area that attracts them. If they're dissatisfied, communicate to them what your financial situation is. See if they can hang on until things improve. Do what you can to get them through the down time now and keep them with you.

It's not "one size fits all" when it comes to motivation. Get to know your employees this week and you'll be able to give the right prescription for motivation!

Points to Ponder

1. What motivates you at work? Is it money? If not, then what?

2. Think back on an achievement at work that was remarkable. Was it more important that you were recognized or did you think pay should be involved?

3. How are you at giving positive feedback? Do you make it a point to recognize people for "just doing their job?" If not, why?

4. If you could never afford incentive pay again, would you be prepared to reward people regularly with intangibles? Would that be difficult for you?

5. Can you identify the "sweet spots" for your three best employees? Do you ever motivate them in those areas?

> Worst manager of the year award goes to a sup of a customer service call center I worked at a few years ago. Of course call centers can be a challenge to operate and manage, but her managerial skills severely lacked ethical and fair values. She assumed that micro managing and using scare-tactics would somehow boost our productivity, in reality it reduced the teams morale and tenure. She criticized heavily for low-performance and lacked improvement plans. She had zero interpersonal, logical, and decision-making talents. She made lives miserable. My cubicle felt like a padded cell with no door. I couldn't even imagine her personality! At first, I thought I wanted a career, it turned out I just wanted paychecks.... after a while I wanted out!
>
> C. H.

Chapter 8 – Get A Grip!

I've beat the topic of evil bosses to death in previous writings so I won't go there now, but we need to take a look at one of the most common behaviors of toxic bosses: emotional outbursts (a nice way to say "freaking out.")

All of us have probably experienced the stress of working around yellers and screamers, but maybe a look at why it happens would be helpful. Recently a colleague of mine, Melinda Ostermeyer, shared a concept with me surrounding an interesting part of the brain known as the **Amygdala.** This almond-shaped (yes, Amygdala is Greek for an almond) is the part of the brain that regulates the flow of Cortisol and Adrenaline which as you may know helps operate the "fight or flight" syndrome in us when we face danger.

Here's how it works. When you're operating normally without stress, your brain is capable of processing multiple "bits" of data, which helps us make rational decisions. As our stress increases, the Amygdala flows more Cortisol and Adrenaline into our brain, which has the effect of limiting the amount of "bits" we can handle. When we hit maximum stress, there is so much Cortisol and Adrenaline in us that we can only make ONE decision (which of course in the caveman days told us to run from the dinosaur or pick up a weapon and fight it.) These chemicals can stay flowing in our brain for up to 18 minutes, which is why it's easy to keep triggering this reaction if stress continues.

So what's the point?

Think of how you react to others when you're stressed out. Do you snap at them? Yell at them? Even physically abuse them? If you know what tends to trigger your Amygdala, then begin taking steps to either avoid or manage it. When that particular situation arises, take a few deep breaths. If someone in particular has a way of pushing your buttons, either avoid them or at least limit your interactions with them, particularly when you're already a little stressed. More than anything, realize how powerful the Amygdala can be and be mindful of it as you interact with others during your day.

Do you remember the "boat people" from the late 1970s and early 1980s? These refugees from Vietnam crossed the Pacific Ocean in droves trying to escape the repression of the Khmer Rouge using overloaded rickety boats. This was no easy journey. Many of the boats were lost at sea and countless refugees drowned. A group later studied the reasons why some boats made it and others didn't. What they found was interesting: on each both that made it, there was one calm person in the boat who was able to manage their own Amygdala. When they were calm in the face of crises, all others around them responded accordingly. Rather than throw the oars overboard and panic when there was trouble, these folks calmly took stock of the situation and stayed in control.

Are you the calm person in your boat? People around you will be drawn to you if you can be the calm and rational person when stress or problems arise. They won't be impressed when you start yelling and screaming. Anyone can panic and freak out. Carefully manage your Amygdala and you'll go a long way to maximizing your people skills!

Points to Ponder

1. Have you ever worked for a "screamer?" How did it make you feel when they flew off the handle?

2. Do you have "hot buttons?" Can you tell when someone is getting ready to push them? How do you handle that?

3. Think about a person you know who is calm under pressure. Are they any different from you? If not, can you emulate their ability to control their emotions?

4. Have you ever been the "calm person in the boat?" If so, what steps did you take to get there? Can you repeat that performance?

> "The worst manager/boss I ever had was a lawyer. He was rude and always tried to make his employees feel small. He would never return calls and left us to fend off angry clients and he also had a back door he would slip out frequently and leave us to explain to the client (who had an appointment) that all of a sudden, he was gone! He would request memos be done a certain way, then change him mind, mark it up and throw it back at us! Needless to say, I only worked there about a month!"
>
> B. T.

Chapter 9 – Do You Have A Life?

"Those kids didn't come in your seabag!"

You probably don't know this, but I did a 15-year career in the Navy. Many things stand out in my mind from that experience, but the line above is at that top of the list.

Of course any one in the Navy can expect a career that includes transfers every three years or so, but as you might imagine, it's not always easy. As families grow, sailors begin to wrestle with uprooting kids from school, deployments where they might be away from home for six to twelve months at a time. It can be a challenge. One plea for mercy though never worked – at least while I was in. Never tell the detailer (the person who assigns you) that the transfer will affect the family – the response could be: "Those kids didn't come in your seabag!"

Now I'll grant you this didn't happen all the time, and of course the mission of defending the country requires sacrifice, but there's no denying that a person's mind would be consumed by thoughts of family, particularly if they were deployed. The same rule applies in any workplace. Your employees have outside concerns. They can't just turn off their personal lives at work.

In many of the workshops I do, we get started with an icebreaker activity called "Little-Known Facts" where each participant shares something about themselves (nothing embarrassing of course) that few people, if any would know. The teaching point is to make the case that knowing something more than just superficial information makes a manager seem more responsive and interested in their workers.

Does it work? ABSOLUTELY! If a manager shows interest and appears relevant to their staff, they'll get much more in terms of productivity, positive attitude, and support.

People spend their most productive hours in the workplace. Believe it or not, people do have a life outside the office. No matter what you do or say, you won't EVER become more important to them than those concerns – so don't think you can be. But do you have to coddle and baby everyone? Must you set aside your business goals to ensure their private life is working?

Of course not! You're their manager not their mother. All I'm saying is to consider what a person is going through and be a little sensitive and compassionate. If an employee is experiencing stress at home and their normally good performance is slipping, show them some concern and be patient. If they've been a stellar performer before, they'll get back to that level.

Being a leader requires sacrifice and development on your part. If you're not an empathetic person by nature, try to develop those skills. And don't be fake about it – your employees won't buy it. Nothing makes you look more stupid than frantically calling to find out why an employee is late to work and then telling them you were worried they might have been in a car accident. If you're really concerned they aren't there to do your business, tell them that, but don't frame it around concern for well being if you really don't care. Better to develop that compassionate spirit through some personal development.

It's a skill every good leader and manager needs to know!

Points to Ponder

1. Do you know "little known facts" about each of your employees?

2. When an employee is late, are you genuinely concerned for their safety or just angry they aren't there?

3. Are you patient with stellar employees that are in a "slump?" How about your less skilled employees?

"The worst manager I ever worked for was 8 years ago at the company I'm currently working for. She was rude, sarcastic and unapproachable. She didn't give a second thought about embarrassing you in front of your fellow employees. I was so on edge because of this woman that I would go home many nights crying. My performance at work also suffered because of the stress as a result of how I was treated by her. One day I stood up to her (wisely, without making a fool of myself) and this lady now gives me the respect I deserve and I respect her in turn."

T.D.

Chapter 10 – Are You Emotional?

Our ninth principle focuses on intelligence, and I'm not talking about working only with smart people. If we're going to be effective managers and great leaders, we have to look at developing a new type of intelligence – emotional intelligence.

People are emotional beings. Deal with them accordingly.

In a recent Gallup Poll study, data was crunched from 25 years of interviews of one million workers across various sectors. Gallup found that the single most important variable in employee productivity and loyalty is the quality of the relationship between employee and their direct supervisor. We're not talking about familiarity here either – this means a supervisor who really cares.

In another study, Researchers at Harvard took a cross section of graduates from law, medicine and business and followed them for 30 years to identify indicators of success. For the purpose of the study, "Success" was defined by professional achievement in their prospective fields as well as stability in key relationships. The objective was to look at those who were most successful and determine what it was about them that could have predicted their success. Here is what they found: IQ was only about 8-

9% of a predictor of success. In fact, at the highest levels of IQ, there was a negative correlation to future success. Technical skills contributed about the same – only 8-9% of future success could be attributed to them. The winner in this study was Emotional Intelligence, which accounted for more than *twice* IQ & technical skills combined in determining who would be successful!

This really shouldn't be a surprise though. After all, if people are emotional beings, Emotional Intelligence will outplay a prestigious management degree every time. The great news is we can start working this process now! IQ is relatively fixed – that is, at age 16 our levels of IQ become fairly concrete, BUT emotional intelligence can be learned and improved at any age.

I'll give you some strategies to work on shortly, but let's agree to view our employees as emotional beings and consider ways to connect with them at that level.

Points to Ponder

1. Do you consider yourself an emotional person? Does that thought scare you?

2. Think about a time where a manager you worked for dealt with you on an emotional level that matched yours. Did that help or hurt the situation?

3. Do you know the difference between sympathy and empathy? If not, look them up on the dictionary. Which of the two do you do more of at work?

4. Can you see where Emotional Intelligence is far superior in developing "people skills?" If not, why?

5. Identify some key areas in your life where you can build emotional intelligence. Can you put together an action plan to develop those? Do you think they can enhance relationships out of work as well? Why or why not?

6. Think back on significant leaders in history and in your own life. Did they maximize Emotional Intelligence?

"My worst manager was actually very recent. This particular one knew nothing! All the responsibilities lied with me. I had to do everything and yet she received all the credit. If there was a part of my position that was unclear to be I could not go to here for help I had to call the support line. Our numbers were up and the office was running smoothly until I had to be out for surgery for 8 weeks mind you. I started receiving calls on every aspect of the office. When I returned I begin to post out for other positions and now I can say that I finally got OUT."

S. S.

Chapter 11 – Are You A Know-It-All?

When I was in the Navy, there was a certain person we all knew no matter where we were stationed. This person seemed to know exactly what was going on and specifically how to solve problems and give advice. This person was known as the "Sea Lawyer."

Now the problem with the "Sea Lawyer" was not that they knew things, it was that they THOUGHT they knew things. Their information came from bits and pieces of rumor and filled in with advice from others and past experiences. It usually meant the advice they gave you was believable enough for you to take action on, but generally the wrong information.

Is it possible to know everything there is to know about management? Maybe. After all, there are "Sea Lawyer" equivalents all over corporate America. Someone will always jump up to offer you advice. There are of course numerous books on the subject – just take a walk through the management aisle of any large bookstore. Nearly every celebrity and academic has a perspective. You can also take classes, seminars, and workshops. It's safe to say there are more than enough resources available to you.

Is it enough though?

Absolutely not! No matter how many classes you take and how many books you read, you'll never know everything there is to know about management. Think about it. You are managing human beings. No computer system can match the intelligence possessed in the human brain. No robotic equipment can adapt as quickly to manual labor as a human can. No artificial intelligence programmer can factor in the multiple emotions a human has. There's no way you'll ever figure it all out. How then can anyone say they don't need to continually learn about management?

I'm also intrigued by folks who tell me in workshop critiques that the course was too basic. (*"A good course for entry-level managers, but not for senior people."*) At what point do we put off the fundamentals and search for new answers? How about NEVER!

A few years ago I read a story in the *USA Today* describing the rise in NBA talent from Europe and the eroding skill levels of U.S. born players. Every expert interviewed in the article said the same thing: European players drill endlessly on the fundamentals: dribbling, passing, and shooting. U.S. players skip fundamentals, focusing on flashy individualism. Current NBA superstars increasingly hail from overseas – the fundamentals work!

So how do we focus on management and leadership fundamentals? Start by committing yourself to an hour of reading and study per day.

Attend workshops with an open mind. Get yourself assigned to a coach or a mentor. Make a conscious effort to grow in your abilities.

Your hard work will pay off if you really put forth the effort.

Points to Ponder

1. Do people around you consider you a "know it all?" If so, is that a positive trait?

2. Are you proficient in the fundamentals of management? Would additional training help you?

3. Have you ever used a mentor? What about a coach? If so, was the experience beneficial?

4. Would you ever consider getting a mentor or coach? Why or why not?

5. Do you function now as a mentor or coach? If so, how is that experience for you?

6. Are you ready to develop a personal and professional development plan? Are you committed to sticking with it? (if so, see the recommended reading in Appendix II)

"The worst manager I ever worked for was at my last job. She just flat out lied, she'd promise you a raise and then turn around and say I never promised you a raise. Later she'd come back and say ok. I did promise you one but I'm just not giving it to you, I just said that so you'd stay. She would show up for work in the morning in her housecoat and slippers. She also told your personal business and she was never at work when you needed her. Her excuse was she could say, do, and act as she pleases because she also owned the place."

Y. E.

Chapter 12 – I'm Not You!

People are individuals with unique needs, desires, personalities, and motivation. A "one size fits all" approach won't work for you.

We covered this back in Principle #1. If you believe that principle, then #11 should work for you. You have to treat individuals individually.

I don't know about you, but it's nearly impossible for me to buy a suit off the rack. My jacket size is a hair under 46 Short and pants around a 38-inch waist with a 30-inch inseam. That's not a common size. Now I have two choices. I could work hard to change my body type – which would not be easy but probably a good thing with diet and exercise, OR, I could have the larger suit off the rack tailored. Right now, that's a more attractive choice. When it's finished, the suit works pretty well – not too tight, not too loose.

Motivating and dealing with your people is the same way. How could you possibly use a "one size fits all" approach successfully? The beauty of studying organizational and human behavior is the diversity! It's a field that you'll never master – how could you? It always changes and you never know what kinds of people will enter your life (or your department.)

Take a look at diagram on the next page.

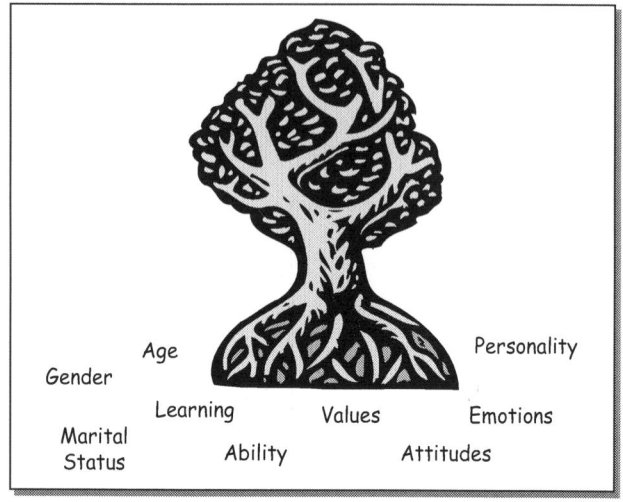

Figure 4

Figure 4 shows a tree, which of itself really isn't remarkable, although it's beautiful and beneficial. The key for a tree is its root system. For human beings, the root system is made up of many components: age, gender, marital status, learning style, ability, values, attitudes, personality, and emotions. Everyone has them in varying quantities and uses them differently.

If the root system is different for everyone, then it stands to reason that the tree would be different as well. Again, one size would not fit all when it comes to managing and leading. You simply have to be flexible and commit to constant learning.

There is a benefit to this kind of diversity though. Think about how different people then view a problem differently. The solutions you can't fathom might be easy for someone with a different root system. Your challenge will be to listen and ask good question. The solutions to your biggest problems might be right in your midst. Tune in and you'll be pleasantly surprised!

Points to Ponder

1. Take a look inside yourself – what does your root structure look like?

2. Think about three figures from history – could people have made incorrect assumptions based on how they appeared on the outside? What do you suppose their root structures looked like?

> "As far as the worst manager I've ever worked for I guess it would have to be, a manager that wanted to be everyone's friend and did not know how to be their leader. It's was frustrating because nothing ever really got done because she was to concern with upsetting the employees and worried that they would not like her anymore. I felt like I was pretty much on my own, as did most of us there. Eventually upper management caught on and got rid of her in that position and move her somewhere else within the company."
>
> A. D.

Chapter 13 – Throw in the Towel!

This final principle might be for more people than you think.

Being The Boss is not for everyone. If you see that it's not a good role for you, do everyone a favor and get out. Your knowledge, skills, and experience will be a better fit elsewhere.

Does that shock you? It shouldn't. I know plenty of people who moved into management roles simply because it the next logical step in career development. They never gave any thought towards whether it was a good fit or not. In fact, many managers I know never thought the "people" stuff would be so difficult and time consuming.

I write about management, teach on management, and do plenty of consulting on management, but I learned back in 1995 that management was not for me. I didn't have the heart or the stomach for it. It wasn't a good fit with my skills or personality. I have however found a calling in what I do now. Do I consider myself a failure or a hypocrite? Absolutely not. I was wise to get out when I could.

But let's talk about you? Can you identify the reason you're in management now? Is it a good fit? Are you in it for the right reasons? Do you love people?

If you can answer these questions honestly, you'll have your answer. I can show you all the tips and techniques but unless you're really committed to being an effective manager and a great leader, they won't work.

Perhaps the first order of business for you is to do some soul searching. When you've come up with your answer, why not commit to the following strategy?

1. Commit to making the change – just baby steps for now. Pick one or two of the principles and begin working on it.

2. Don't get discouraged. Any habit is hard to break – beware of the self-fulfilling prophecy – it will happen.

3. Commit right now, today here at this meeting to move forward. Pick a partner or get a coach and hold yourself accountable.

4. Think about this as an investment in your own future, your own professional development. Your hard work now can solidify you as a great manager and a valuable resource. You may change lives as a result.

5. Be Positive: A recent study by insurance carrier MetLife determined that sales people who were optimistic sold 29% more insurance in their first year and 130% more in their second year than did pessimists.

So that's it. Simple, but not simplistic. None of these are earth shattering – just simple things you can do, baby-steps at a time, to make a difference as a manager. If you want to be a better manager, a better leader, even a better family member, get busy and work the principles.

I'm convinced that working each of the first 11 principles will get you noticed by your employees and your boss (in a good way!) If you choose to really get serious about Principle #12, everyone will notice. If you're in management for the wrong reason, get out! If you're in it for the right reason, then stay in but get deadly serious about doing it right. I'm excited to see and hear about the remarkable things you do in your management role.

Now get off the bench and back in the game!

Develop People

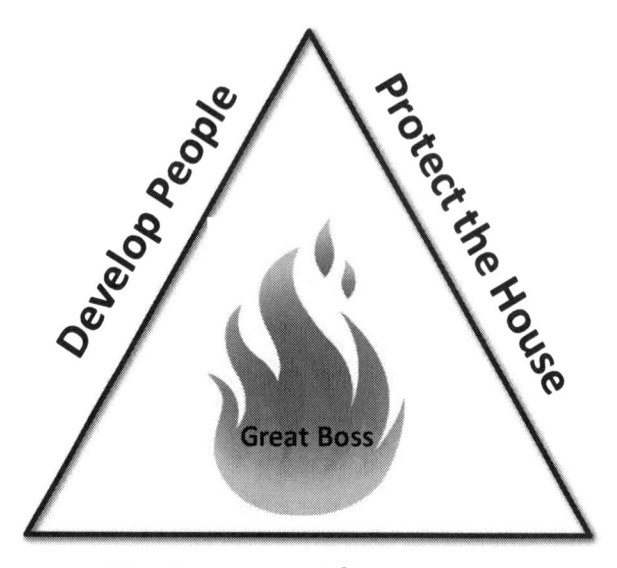

Protect the House

Great Boss

Fix Systems/Processes

About the Author

Mack Munro is Founder and CEO of **Boss Builders** and is an experienced speaker, consultant, and coach who has worked with executive and management teams in companies of all types, sizes, and industries in the USA and abroad. He is the author of *How to Win at Performance Management)* and 11 other business books.

He holds a Master of Arts degree in Organizational Leadership from Chapman University and a Bachelor of Science degree in Health Care Management from Southern Illinois University He is a qualified facilitator of the Myers-Briggs Type Indicator® and has also written and developed a number of personality and behavioral assessments and online tools.

Mack's background is primarily in Healthcare, Manufacturing, Consulting, Information Technology, Entrepreneurship, Leadership & Management, and Marketing. His typical clients come from these areas.

Prior to starting his company, Mack created training and professional development programs at U.T. Medical Group, Inc. in Memphis, TN,

Holy Cross Hospital in Silver Spring, MD, and Contract Services Association of America in Arlington, VA. Mack has been an adjunct Professor of Business and Management at Vincennes University in Bremerton, WA and Crichton College in Memphis, TN. He a retired United States Navy dental technician who served tours in Australia, Guam, Long Beach, California, and Bremerton, Washington.

Mack's clients include Pratt & Whitney, UTC Research, Pitney Bowes, Munters Corporation, Connecticut Online Computer Center, Bridgestone, CU Direct, numerous Federal agencies, and all 4 branches of the United States Military. He has delivered keynotes to groups and associations around the country and internationally, and is a regular speaker at the Society for Human Resource Management (SHRM) state and local chapter meetings.

He has been featured as a career expert on radio, television, and printed and electronic media, including a monthly column in *Men's Fitness* magazine.

You can reach Mack for speaking engagements on his blog at:

www.MackMunro.com

Mack Munro
P.O. Box 75
Vanleer, TN 37181
(931) 221-2988
Mack@TheBossBuilders.com

About Boss Builder Academy

Boss Builders provides turnkey training and development solutions to better prepare **The Boss** to fix systems and processes and develop their team. Our proven process allows us to partner with you and provide the structure, systems, tools, and techniques to develop a management team of any size, even one with just a single learner! Here's how it works:

Step #1: Assess The Boss: This is done through the use of our proprietary online assessment. Each manager is evaluated on the Focus Factors for the particular organization's management role. The boss's immediate supervisor will provide this information in partnership with us. The Boss Builder Guide will work with the individual in helping them more closely align themselves with the required Focus Factors.

Step #2: Basic Training: The Boss will take a series of video-based, self-paced training sessions. These lessons are short and provide easy-to-adopt tools, models and techniques.

Step #3: Development: After Step #2, The Boss will then participate in onsite or virtual Management Roundtable® sessions where they have an open-forum, facilitator-led and peer participative sessions to wrestle with specific issues. This ties in the learning from Step #2 with practical advice from seasoned management experts.

Step #4: Re-assess The Boss: After completing the basic trainin, The Boss will be reevaluated with our online assessment tool and also at the end of all phases of Basic Training assessed on progress towards **Competencies**. Upon successful evaluation, The Boss will enter Phase #2 where the cycle repeats with more advanced leadership learning.

Who is "The Boss?"

"The Boss" is the term we give to anyone in a position of supervision. The goal is to be a Great Boss!

Great bosses master the three critical components of the job

- Fixing Systems and Processes
- Protecting "The House"
- Developing Talent

Fixing Systems and Processes
These tasks are where managers or supervisors are the most comfortable. It's probably why you hired them. Without attention here, the business is going to struggle. Unfortunately, there is far more to the role than these tasks though.

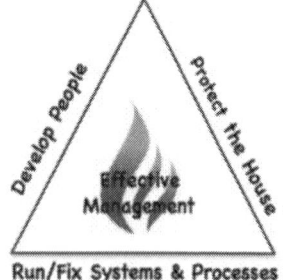

Protecting "The House"
The Boss needs to look out for hazards, from safety issues all the way to HR liability issues. It's not glamorous but it's absolutely critical.

Developing People

This is the most important role and the one where most bosses are least competent and confident. When the boss devotes time to developing the team, the entire operation becomes stronger.

Boss Competencies

Being The Boss means you've mastered a number of competencies (when you think of competencies, think of someone being incompetent. Incompetent means you are not competent in the competencies, or core requirements of the job.) We've identified the following competencies:

Boss Competencies for Phase 1: *Getting Started as The Boss*
- Accountability
- Building Trust
- Coaching
- Written Communication
- Oral Communication
- Developing Others
- Listening
- Managing Performance
- Organizational Communication
- Providing Direction
- Providing Motivational Support
- Technical Credibility

Boss Competencies for Phase 2: *Growing as The Boss*
- Change Management
- Conflict Management
- Continual Improvement

Decision Making
Emotional Intelligence
Getting Results
Interpersonal Skills
Solving Problems
Systems Thinking

Boss Competencies for Phase 3: *Being The Boss*
Analytical Thinking
Delegation
Empowering Others
Flexibility
Influencing Others
Meeting Ethical Standards
Managing Risk
Negotiation
Partnering/Networking
Political Skill
Thinking Strategically

Evaluating The Boss

The New Boss will be evaluated at the beginning and end of the program by their manager in partnership with a Boss Builders Guide. The assessment will be done online and measure progress in our proprietary 360 survey.

Boss Basic Training

Basic Training involves transferring knowledge around the necessary skills for being The Boss. These 48 topics are short (5 – 7 minutes max), practical, and absolutely imperative for The Boss to master.

Phase 1: Getting Started as The Boss
1. What is My Job as The Boss?
2. How to "Protect the House"
3. Myths About Being The Boss
4. How to Look and Act Like The Boss
5. How to Manage Former Peers
6. How to Think Like The Boss
7. How to Communicate Like The Boss
8. How to Communicate With Your Department and Organization
9. How to Communicate With Individuals
10. How to Build Rapport
11. How to Get Better Performance from Your Team
12. How to Diagnose Poor Performance
13. How to Motivate Unmotivated People
14. How to Diagnose Focus Problems
15. How to Help People Develop
16. How to Give Positive Feedback
17. How to Give Negative (Corrective) Feedback
18. How NOT to Screw Up Feedback
19. How to Be a Good Coach
20. How to Coach for Skill and Focus

Phase 2: Growing as The Boss
21. How to Be a Systems and Process Thinker
22. How to Create and Use a Flowchart
23. How to Create and Use a Fishbone Diagram
24. How to Solve Complicated Problems
25. How to Make Better Use of Data in Solving Problems
26. How to Explain Your Problem or Solution using Dollar Figures
27. How to Make a Better Decision
28. How to Be Emotionally Intelligent

29. How to Manage Conflict
30. How to Manage Change
31. How to Document Performance
32. How to Have Career and Development Conversations

Phase 3: Being The Boss
33. How to Systemize Your Department
34. How to Plan and Prioritize
35. How to Set Goals and Strategies
36. How to Successfully Communicate Upwards
37. How to Delegate Successfully
38. How to Adjust Your Political (Organizational) Attitude
39. How to Navigate Your Organization's Politics
40. How to Negotiate Effectively
41. How to Value and Leverage Diversity
42. How to Build and Run a Synergistic Team
43. How to Build Your Bench (and Replace Yourself)
44. How to Create Healthy Habits for Yourself
45. How to Take Next Steps as The Boss

FAQ

Why Do You Believe a Bad Boss Is Better Than a Leader?

We don't. What we're saying is that the opposite of a boss isn't necessarily a leader. What we want to do is build a foundation of basic skills that will enable somebody who is new to the role of being the boss to be successful. Once they are successful, then the process of leadership development can begin. But just the blanket comparison we believe is wrong.

Why Do You Keep Referring to Managers as The Boss?

We do this because most people refer to their direct supervisor as their boss. The Boss could be anyone from a team lead, to a supervisor, to a manager, to a director, and even a VP-level person. Basically it's the person who guides you and tells you what to do on a daily basis. We just narrow that term down to be "The Boss."

So How Do You Create Good Bosses?

We begin by referencing **31 basic competencies** that any good manager would have to master to be successful. What we do in our program is have the newly appointed manager take a self-assessment of their skills and abilities around those competencies. We also have their boss do the same assessment on them. In that way we partner with you to develop your managers. This gives us a foundation of what we have to work with.

Okay So Now You've Assessed Where They Are, What Happens Next?
We have divided our program into three phases, with each phase lasting around a month or so. We call these *Phases Getting Started As The Boss, Growing As The Boss,* and *Being The Boss*. Each phase builds on the last phase and what it does is gives the new boss the foundation to be able to add to their repertoire of Knowledge and Skills. The final phase, *Being The Boss*, is very strategic and enables the new boss to start acting and being successful on a larger stage.

How Do You Run Your Classes?
Our preference is always face to face and in a group setting, but we know that's not always possible, feasible, or affordable. What we've done is broken down the topics into **45 short videos**, about 7 to 9 Minutes in duration, with a workbook where they can take notes. The video instructor is our **Founder and CEO Mack Munro** who takes them through the materials. They can watch these on their own schedule at their own time using either a desktop computer, their mobile device, or tablet.

Where Do You Get the Management Training Models and Techniques? How Do We Know They Actually Work?
Mack Munro has been a management development practitioner for over 20 years. In his travels and research, he's seen the best and worst management practices. The materials, models, techniques, and behaviors are based on his experience and we guarantee they work.

But Isn't There More to Growing as The Boss Than Just Watching a Bunch of Videos?

Absolutely! The real value of our Boss Builders program is that after each phase and throughout each phase, the new boss meets virtually or in person with a designated, certified **Boss Builder Guides**. Our guides are experienced in various areas of industry and human resources and draw upon their years of experience to answer questions and go through the material with the boss who is in our program. These one-on-one meetings or group Roundtable meetings (done in person or through interactive webinars) are the opportunities our students have to ask questions, get clarification, or bring their real-world issues to the table and get guided answers.

Do We Have Any Part in This Program or Does Boss Builders Handle It All?

Absolutely! You can't possibly outsource management development to a vendor like us and expect it to work. We partner with you by having you evaluate the progress of your bosses. We share the survey data with the immediate supervisor and form a triangle of knowledge, the boss, the boss's boss, and the Boss Builder guide. Between the three people in this exchange, we can communicate effectively and ensure that we are providing the right type of guidance to make your boss successful in your own company. Additionally, we recommend that you begin to work with your new boss to find mentors internally to help guide them further in their journey.

What Happens When They Get Through All the Videos?

Upon completion of the video series, we want to reevaluate the progress using the same survey that we begin the program with. What we look for here is demonstrated growth in the actions, skills, and competencies, if your new boss appears to be successful, we will recommend leadership development as probably the next step. The good news is, as part of our program you will have access to the 45 initial videos as well as access to our *BossFlix®* Library where we present short topics that are very specific to issues that managers write in and ask us about. This provides on-demand learning whenever that newly designated boss needs help.

Do You Provide Leadership Development?
Yes. We recommend however that if you are serious about growing your boss to that level, you use a different process then what a lot of vendors will offer. We recommend the use of a **certified coach** as well as our 360-degree surveys to enable your successful boss to start taking on greater challenges and developing leadership behaviors. And our experience, these are not done well through classes or group events. He's our one-on-one areas where an individual can get focused attention to hone their abilities to a razor's edge. We can provide this for you.

You Mentioned Just the Videos, Do You Also Do Classroom Training with These Topics?
Yes. We have instructors that will come on site and provide the same skills that you see in the videos in a classroom environment. With that venue, we are able to do more skills practice and simulations with groups which enables them to get more rapid transfer of Knowledge and Skills. We are flexible and that we can do these in short segments which minimizes the time away from the job.

When we come on site, we also save you a great deal of travel dollars. With any of our on-site programs, we also offer access to the video series and the *BossFlix®* series when you have completed our classroom program.

Ok We're Interested! How Do We Get Started?
Call us at (931) 221-2988 and we'll do a quick call to get a scope of what you want done and then send you a quote. You can also email us at lisa@thebossbuilder.com.

That's Scary. Before I Waste My Time with This, Can You Tell Me How Much It Costs?
The cost depends on the scope of your project. Let me just assure you though, we provide, the most effective, most efficient, and MOST AFFORDABLE management training in the industry. Trust me, you won't be frightened by the cost!

We want to work with you!

Go to *www.TheBossBuilders.com* to get more information and view a sample video!

BOSSBUILDERS

Additional Resources from Boss Builders

We have two additional options available to help you, the busy and stressed HR professional improve the competence and confidence of your company's managers.

Option #1: Our Onsite *Driving Results*® Instructor-Led Workshops

***Driving Results*® Onsite Workshops** are the most efficient way to train a small group of Bosses (between 10 and 30 participants) if you prefer live training at a location of your choosing.

This program, if delivered from start to finish, is four-days long. We can deliver it for you in half or one-day increments if you like.

Benefits:

- Interactive training and the opportunity for live skills practice.

- Opportunity to weave current participant challenges into the workshop.

- No travel expenses for attendees.
  If you're interested in us bringing our training onsite to your organization, we are happy to oblige. Here is our standard course offering. Scroll to the very bottom for pricing.
  Driving Results **Onsite Instructor-Led Program**

Purpose:

The main purpose of this training is to better prepare people managers in addressing the many employee issues that arise day to day in their busy schedule.

- Working and communicating with employees.
- Resolving conflicts before they become larger issues.
- Developing the performance of individuals and teams.
- Improving systems, processes, and decisions.

This program will be delivered onsite and facilitated by one of our certified, experienced Boss Builders professional trainers. You will have an opportunity to chat with them before your session to address any nuances of the group and get a chance to ask them any questions.

Driving Results is modularized and can be delivered end-to-end in three days or broken up into half-day, one-day, or two-day events. Training is invoiced at a per-day or, when applicable, half-day rate.

Driving Results Program Description

The ***Driving Results*** program is designed to teach basic management skills in an interactive format through the use of assessments, lecture, discussion, skills practice, and video clips. It consists of the following classes that can be delivered individually or in modules over a three-day period.

Module 1: Embracing Your Role as The Boss
Duration: 1 hour

Description:
The role of a manager is challenging considering the numerous changes you'll face. To be successful we need to balance the needs of the people against the needs of the organization. To do this requires new skills. In this module, participants will learn how to:

- Embrace your role as The Boss.

- Navigate the changes in your role such as managing former peers and associates.

- Identify the right style to use in driving performance

Module 2: Building Relationships for Results
Duration: 4 hours

Description:
Building Relationships for Results is designed to show you the importance of good communication, your default behavioral style, and how to build rapport with others. In this module, participants will learn how to:

- Develop better emotional intelligence.

- Improve their communication styles.

- Eliminate communication barriers and personal biases.

- Embrace the strengths and weaknesses of their behavioral styles.

- Minimize the worst and maximize the best of interpersonal conflict.
- Work to achieve win-win solutions.
- Take charge of harmful emotions.
- Be assertive while showing empathy.

Module 3: Driving Results
Duration: 6 hours

Description:
Driving Results is designed to give you tools and techniques to become an effective manager of performance. In this module, participants will learn how to:

- Use diagnostic tools such as the *3-Legged Stool of Great Performance*™ and the *M-4 Development Model*™.
- Diagnose performance issues through the use of effective feedback.
- Coach employees for success using the *PULL*™ methodology.
- Delegate more effectively.
- Diagnose and improve team cohesiveness.
- Facilitate career development conversations.
- Ask better, more effective questions.

Module 4: Engaging Employees
Duration: 2 hours

Description:
Engaging Employees is designed to give you tools and techniques to develop a culture of motivation and engagement In this module, participants will learn how to:

- Define "Engagement" in a practical and useful manner.
- Identify 12 common motivational drivers.
- Create an environment where engagement thrives.
- Take action to minimize restraining forces on a culture of engagement.

Module 5: Improving Systems and Processes
Duration: 3 hours

Description:
Improving Systems and Processes is designed to give you tools and techniques to better run your department and be seen as a critical thinker. In this module, participants will learn how to improve systems and processes through the use of:

- Gap Analysis
- Root Cause Analysis
- Flowcharting
- The Fishbone Diagram

- Brainstorming
- The Affinity Diagram
- Run Charts
- Change Perception Model™

Module 6: Planning and Prioritizing
Duration: 4 hours

Description:
Planning and Prioritizing is designed to give you tools and techniques to manage more effectively by looking strategically at data and situations and make more informed decisions. In this module, participants will learn how to improve planning and prioritizing through the use of:

- The Circular Causal Loop
- The Cost of the Problem™
- What Would Have to Be True? Model
- The Pre-Mortem

Module 7: Your Power and Influence
Duration: 2 hours

Description:
Your Power and Influence is designed to give you new data regarding your own personal power and your most comfortable styles of influence. In this module, participants will learn how to:

- Identify personal power and influence.
- Develop strategies to grow these bases in an organization.

Module 8: Navigating Organizational Politics
Duration: 2 hours

Description:
Navigating Organizational Politics is designed to give you tools and techniques to better leverage your power and influence to get your team seen, heard, and respected. In this module, participants will learn how to:

- Identify the correct attitude towards organizational politics.
- Recognize the factors that give politics an unfavorable reputation.
- Take active steps to leverage politics for professional success.

Option #2: *Driving Results®* Curriculum License and Purchase

License and Materials
This license gives company the right to purchase and deliver our Driving Results workshops to your team. The license stays with your organization for as long as you like and does NOT transfer to any individual if they leave your company. Former employees can purchase a license in their new organization if they choose. This protects your investment.

The license gives you access to a robust instructor guide which includes a slide-by-slide video demonstration with suggestions on delivery techniques. You'll also have access to any product updates via a dedicated learning portal. A certified Boss Builder facilitator can be onsite to walk you through set-up or co-instruct with your trainers on a per-day basis. This rate is available when you open your quote as an option.

Each attendee must purchase a workbook and assessment which is priced per-user in the quote. These will be marked up in a class as there are many fill-in-the-blank areas.

Notes and Reflections – Week #1

Start

Continue

Change

Stop

Notes and Reflections – Week #2

Start

Continue

Change

Stop

Notes and Reflections – Week #3

Notes and Reflections – Week #4

Notes and Reflections – Week #5

Start

Continue

Change

Stop

Notes and Reflections – Week #6

Start

Continue

Change

Stop

Notes and Reflections – Week #7

Start

Continue

Change

Stop

Notes and Reflections – Week #8

Start

Continue

Change

Stop

Notes and Reflections – Week #9

Start

Continue

Change

Stop

Made in the USA
Columbia, SC
15 March 2019